M000087096

40 Days Alone with God
Meditations for Renewal III

Roy J. Jones Jr.

Dr. Roy P. Jones, Jr.

Copyright 2018 © Roy P. Jones, Jr.
ISBN 9781720292746

TABLE OF CONTENTS

FOREWORD

Examining the life of Jesus reveals to us the natural rhythm of life, the balance between solitude and action. The mystics don't have it all right when there is sometimes an over emphasis of solitude at the expense of action, but neither do the social activists have it all right when there is an over emphasis on action at the expense of solitude. The right perspective is when there is a mixture of the two.

Dr. Jones' work, *40 Days Alone with God: Meditations for Renewal III*, correctly assumes that if the church is to have the power of the Early Church as witnessed in the Acts of the Apostles, we must effectively blend solitude and action, that our solitude bears heavily upon our work in the world and our ability to withstand the pressures that come with life. Action vs. solitude is a false dichotomy that must be torn down if the church is going to have the power it once had. Dr. Jones tears it down by placing an emphasis on prayer in his life, and by publishing this devotional from himself and other Christian leaders.

The Devotionals are an invitation to pray, a discipline that is essential for the Christian, where its lack has led powerlessness, and where it is plentiful leads to an infusion of the spirit. I am not surprised Dr. Jones would publish a devotional. His life has certainly exemplified the importance of prayer and the subsequent fruits that are derived from it.

So, as you read, let the spirit of prayer and solitude capture you. As it does, I pray that you will see it as an indispensable discipline as you navigate life and try to make a difference. I leave you these words from Henri Nouwen, "If you start with community and want to be faithful to community, you have to realize what binds us together is not mutual comparability or common tasks, but God. In order to stay in touch with that call to community, we always have to return to solitude."

Rev. Darryl R. Williams
Senior Pastor
St. Stephen AME Church
Detroit, MI

ACKNOWLEDGEMENTS

In alphabetical order, let me note my gratitude to the efforts of the following preachers and laity who helped to write meditations for this book: Rev. Priscilla Adams, Rev. Ina Broomfield, Rev. Melvin Butler, Sister Elaine Campbell, Rev. D'Andrea Daniels, Sister Tammie Dennis, Rev. Jeffery Fields, Rev. Dr. Eddie Fleming, Rev. Dr. Paul Flowers, Rev. Alexia Ford, Rev. Carlton Gibson, Rev. Sharon Adair-Harden, Rev. Daniel Johnson, Rev. Diana Kirk, Rev. Dr. Gene Moore, Rev. Gregory Nettles, Rev. Kurbe Newsom, Rev. Elliot Robinson, Rev. Dr. Derrick Thorpe, Rev. Carolyn Williams, Rev. John Williams, and Brother Jeaune Yarde.

I praise God for the churches, pastors and Christians across the nation who shared their time and talents with me to encourage me in ministry. I thank God for my Pastor, mentor, and friend Rev. William D. Watley, Ph.D., who inspires me through his preaching, teaching, leadership, and writing.

I am also grateful to Janice Armstrong and Princess Hill for their editing and formatting of this book.

DEDICATION

I dedicate this book to my wife Angela, my four daughters, Kemyasha, Atavia, Olivia, and Iona, and my granddaughter Naami. They have been very supportive in my ministry and for that I am eternally grateful.

INTRODUCTION

Everyone goes through something in life. It is important that we are encouraged no matter what we are facing. Our time alone with God in prayer and in His Word is very important in maintaining our sanity. Our devotional time will give us courage to complete each day, as well as finishing strong with the right attitude, and with faith to start a new day with the right attitude.

40 Days Alone with God: Meditations for Renewal III will give you strength, courage, direction and hopefully peace each day. I was excited about this book when I felt God encouraging me to write and share with others.

This book consists of stories, testimonies, prayers, Scriptures from Psalms and Proverbs, and examples that will give us wisdom, understanding, courage and strength. There is a meditation or devotion for each day for the next 40 days. Enjoy the journey. It is my prayer that you will move forward in whatever God has called you to do. May the Lord Bless and Keep you in His care.

Meditations for Renewal III

DAY 1
Overcoming War and Hunger

Psalm 10:17-18 (NRSV)
"O LORD, you will hear the desire of the meek; you will strengthen their heart, you will incline your ear to do justice for the orphan and the oppressed, so that those from earth may strike terror no more."

War destroys communities and families. People often find themselves struggling to survive. It's one thing to read about bombs dropping daily in Syria. It's another for those who live and work there to see the smoke from their office window while their colleagues have had to leave their apartments because their homes are being destroyed by the bombs in this war zone. For those who were born there, or live there, life has been filled with fear, pain, hunger, lost and destruction.

The besieged region of Eastern Ghouta used to be the food basket of Damascus but the fighting has frightened people away from their vegetable gardens and barley fields. There is a lack of medicine, fuel and food due to the war. Parents skip meals to give the little food they have to their starving children.

For those who work and live in Syria life has been challenging, and so much is out of our control. My heart goes out to this country and to the families that are being destroyed and displaced by war. No child anywhere deserves to be punished with hunger and starvation just because they were born in a war zone. We must pray for their safety and deliverance.

By God's grace, a convoy was sent in to deliver food to more than 27,000 people trapped inside Eastern Ghouta during a brief ceasefire, bringing much-needed relief to desperate families. This relief helped those affected by the war to experience renewal. It gives them a glimpse of hope and peace.

There are times when we must deal with the unexpected. We can find ourselves in places we didn't expect to be or in situations that we can't figure out on our own. We can lose so much rather it be our mistakes or an attack of the enemy.

When we are challenged and even defeated by the world and the wars that may cause us to lack the things that we once had or that we need, remember God has the power to bring us out or turn things around.

Prayer

Lord have mercy upon the people of Eastern Ghouta and all of Syria. Lord, we pray for peace and renewal in that region and in other places that have been affected by war, and hunger. Lord we pray for justice and strength for those who are living in war zones. We pray that those who are leading the battle will cease fire and end terror. In Jesus Name we pray. Amen.

Rev. Dr. Roy Jones, Jr
Executive Minister
Saint Philip AME Church
Atlanta, GA

DAY 2
A Prepared Heart

Psalm 10:17-18 (NKJV)

"Lord, You have heard the desire of the humble; You will prepare their heart; You will cause Your ear to hear, To do justice to the fatherless and the oppressed, That the man of the earth may oppress no more."

As we began to pray, have confidence as David did to know that God helps the poor, and God helps the needy. God has not forgotten you nor will He hide His face from those that call upon His name. You must know that no matter the situations that you are faced with, those that humble themselves will be exalted in due time.

God will send help from above as He sees you in need of justice from the situations that surround you like an enemy. Lean on the Lord when you need help and the Lord will be your leaning posts. When you lean on Him, the Lord will lend His ear in your direction.

God can give justice and render judgement upon those things that bound you. The Lord is the One who can relieve the pressures of life, relieve doubt and discouragement. The Lord will restore you, the Lord will revive and rejuvenate you.

Prayer

Lord, we thank You for what You have already done in our life. Let us continue to seek You in our daily life. Help us to prepare our hearts through studying, praying and meditating on Your Word. Lord, prepare us for what lies ahead and give us strength in times of our own weakness.

Rev. Jeffery Fields
Pastor, New Haven MBC
Camden, AR

DAY 3
A Plea for Justice and Righteousness

Psalm 26:1-3 (NRSV)

"Vindicate me, O LORD, for I have walked in my integrity, and I have trusted in the LORD without wavering. Prove me, O LORD, and try me; test my heart and mind. For your steadfast love is before my eyes, and I walk in faithfulness to you."

Richard Jewell was a thirty-four-year-old security guard in 1996. He was never actually convicted of any crime, but in 1996 he became one of the most infamous men on earth. When a bomb exploded at the Olympic Games in Atlanta, it was Richard Jewell whom the FBI said was the chief suspect in this act of terror.

It seemed that Mr. Jewell had followed the correct procedures when he had seen a suspicious package in the Olympic Village and reported it to the authorities. Shortly after reporting what he had seen, the package exploded, killing one person and injuring more than one hundred others. He became the prime suspect in the bombing, and he was quickly villainized.

He was cleared of any charges in October of that same year, but that was well after he had been found guilty in the court of public opinion. Like many cases of the wrongfully accused and convicted, the Jewell case exhibited several aspects of botched police work.

Too often people are wrongfully accused of crimes that they didn't commit. When people are wrongfully accused for anything, it damages relationships and people. It causes pain and frustration that can be hard to overcome. The good news is that with God's help renewal can take place.

People will fail us. The system will fail us as well. During these turbulent times we must remain faithful. God doesn't abandon us because we are accused or because we have issues. We can still experience the wonder working power of Jesus. God can bring about Justice as we call on Him to rescue and renew us. God is a just and righteous God. God will enable us to bear the pain and disappointment or He will lift us from the burden, sorrow, pain, and disappointment, giving us renewed strength and hope.

Prayer

Thank you, Lord, for renewal. You have proven to vindicate us as you did Richard Jewell. Lord, free all of those who have been wrongly accused or charged with a crime that they didn't commit. We pray for righteousness. God grant justice for your people in Jesus Name. Amen.

Rev. Dr. Roy Jones, Jr.
Executive Minister
Saint Philip AME Church
Atlanta, GA

DAY 4

God the Great Deliverer

Psalm 18:3 (NIV)

"I called to the Lord, who is worthy of praise, and I have been saved from my enemies."

In his extremities, David called to the Lord with a heart of thanksgiving. David found relief in knowing that the Lord heard the voice of his supplication. We need to speak to the Lord with confidence, trust Him with assurance and wait patiently in God to act on your behalf. God will strengthen you to face life's trials.

David's deliverance came straight from the Hand of God. God will break our yokes and will destroy the oppressors from our necks. Trust God for saving power. Praise Him for His marvelous work, the God of my salvation, the God of Glory, and the Lord God Almighty.

I have been saved from my enemies, I will not cower, I will not allow the cords of my enemies to choke me, nor trap me. I am saved in Jesus' arms. The eyes of God never will leave me. I bring honor to God and certainly He will deliver me in the day of trouble.

Prayer

Lord God Almighty, your saving Hands rescue me from deep waters of life, the snares of my enemies, the warring of the mind, sickness, and diseases. In Jesus's name. Amen.

Sister Elaine Campbell
Associate Minister
Saint Philip AME Church
Atlanta, GA

DAY 5
A Desire Worth Seeking After

Psalms 27:1-4 (NIV)

"The LORD is my light and my salvation; whom shall I fear? the LORD is the strength of my life; of whom shall I be afraid? When the wicked, even mine enemies and my foes, came upon me to eat up my flesh, they stumbled and fell. Though an host should encamp against me, my heart shall not fear: though war should rise against me, in this will I be confident. One thing have I desired of the LORD, that will I seek after; that I may dwell in the house of the LORD all the days of my life, to behold the beauty of the LORD, and to enquire in his temple."

We find once again, a Psalm pinned by David... There's no particular reference to a moment in his life that these words were born out of. One can easily infer that it refers to a moment when either Saul or another one of his enemies were seeking to kill him. On another hand, David could have very well wrote had he reflected upon the protecting and preserving grace of the Almighty God.

In this Psalm, David makes several conclusions in the opening verse that seems to set the tone for everything else that follows. First, the Lord is his light and salvation. Second, the Lord is the strength of his life. These are terms that one come to through experiencing God. The overall passage reveals that there were some challenges David had to face but the Lord delivered him.

While facing difficulties, often the desire is to overcome and be delivered. Yet, David proclaims in verse 4, "One thing have I desired of the LORD, that will I seek after; that I may dwell in the house of the LORD all the days of my life, to behold the beauty of the LORD, and to enquire in his temple." In essence, all David desired is to be in the Lord's presence... This is A Desire Worth Seeking After for it helps us to take our focus off our situation and place it upon the one who can handle the situation.

Prayer

Dear Lord, quite often we overload ourselves with difficulties and get bogged down with trying to fight our own battles because we desire deliverance. Thank You for being our light, our salvation, and our strength. Forgive us for trusting more in our own ingenuity and abilities than trusting and leaning upon you. Help us to seek and desire to just be in Your presence that we may learn to lean and depend on Your guidance. Let our lives overflow with the joy of being in Your presence whereby there is light, salvation, and strength. Set within us this desire, a desire worth seeking after, to just be in constant fellowship with you. In Jesus name we pray, Amen.

Rev. Dr. E. J. Fleming, Jr.
Founder/Pastor
Faith Tabernacle Baptist Church
Rosharon, TX

DAY 6
The Land of the Living

Psalm 27:13 (NRSV)
"I believe that I shall see the goodness of the LORD in the land of the living."

The Land of the Living is what we are born into, when we are born to Christian and God-fearing parents or families who take us to church and introduce us early to a living Savior, Jesus Christ. If not, we are introduced to and join with the walking dead, people who are alive, however, only for this world but are bound for eternal death and suffering. The great news is that you can become renewed and join the faith body of The Land of the Living at any time.

In the Jewish tradition, The Land of the Living was the city of Jerusalem and the Jewish Temple. Jerusalem and the Temple represented hope and life. In the land of Canaan, in Jerusalem and in the temple; it was grand to see God's face in the temple of God despite all the obstacles of life. In comparison with the heathens, that were dead in sin, the land of Israel and especially the temple might fitly be called The Land of the Living. Today, the church, or the ecclesia, the body of Christian believers, represents The Land of the Living and brings hope to a dying world.

Heaven alone is that which may truly be called The Land of the Living, where there is no more death and no more dying. The earth is the land of the dying. However, there is nothing more comforting and reassuring than the hope, joy and truth of eternal life. The glory that forecast, forbears, foretells and foretastes the pleasures and goodness of heaven. This keep us from fainting under all the pressures, burdens and challenges of the present world. The NRS translation is good but the KJV really captures the peaks and lows of humanities faith journey. KJV Psalm 27:13 *"I had fainted, unless I had believed to see the goodness of the LORD in the land of the living."*

Prayer

Dear Lord, help us to live according to the proclamation of John the Baptist NRS Matthew 3:2 "Repent, for the kingdom of heaven has come near." And that we must have our permanent address recorded and registered into the book of life so that we, our families and loved ones may reside in The Land of the Living now and forever. Amen

Rev. Daniel W. Johnson
Pastor, Allen Temple AME Church
1123 S. Virginia
Pine Bluff, AR 71601

DAY 7
Start Singing

Psalm 28: 6-7 (NRSV)
"Blessed be the Lord, for he has heard the sound of my pleadings. The Lord is my strength and shield; in him my heart trusts; so, I am helped, and my heart exults, and with my song I give thanks to him."

We have the assurance that God hears our prayers. Whatever distresses that the psalmist was facing in this text, he found the help that he needed in prayer. There was no doubt of the nearness of God. He found God to be accessible and faithful. He was very confident that God was concerned, and that God was in control. He was able to proclaim that God heard his pleadings. God knows all about everything we face. He knows the sound of our voice, as well as the sound of our pleadings, when we are tensed, stressed, or even desperate in prayer.

Be confident that we pray to a God who cares about us, a God who is pleased that we bring everything to him in faith. Trust in the living God who will not turn his back to us. God listens to our prayers and enjoys fellowship with us. Believe that he is going to help you through the storms of life. Believe that God is stronger and bigger than any problem.

Rejoice that we serve a God who gives us new strength every hour, who puts a shield of protection all around us, and who knows the distinctive sound of your voice. You are one of the trillions of human beings on this earth. God has uniquely created and formed you and he intimately knows every sound you make. That's enough right there to get excited and overjoyed that he made us, knows us, cares for us and loves us. So, get a song and start singing. Keep singing. God is worthy of song, praise and thanksgiving!

Prayer

Gracious and Eternal God, we thank you for your loving kindness, and for caring about us. We lift up our voices to you in song. Our trust and our faith are in the living God who comes close to us and reveals that we are never alone. Thank you for an outpouring of peace and strength that comes from you. May we share with others how you have blessed and how you made a way. What a wonder you are O Lord. Blessed be the Lord! In the name of Jesus! Amen.

Rev Janice McCray
Evangelism Ministry
Saint Philip AME Church
Atlanta, GA

DAY 8
From Funeral Clothes to Renewed Purpose

Psalm 30: 1-12 (CEV)

"You changed my mourning into dancing. You took off my funeral clothes and dressed me up in joy so that my whole being might sing praises to you and never stop. Lord, my God, I will give thanks to you forever." – Psalms 30:11,12 (Common English Bible Version)

We often think about renewal coming from a conscious decision to make a change. Whether it's through New Year resolutions, fasting or goal setting, renewal often comes as the result of us starting a journey. However, renewal may also come from an unlikely source...illness.

When we are struck with an illness or disease, we can be forced to face our mortality. The reality that we are only on Earth for a season comes clearly into focus. It's often during these times that we truly contemplate who and what are important in our lives and the work that is yet to be done. We welcome the chance for a second chance, but we must know where to turn for renewal.

This Psalm reminds us of the importance of exalting and praising the Lord at all times. Even when it looks like our health has failed and we are not long for this world, don't stop praising and crying out to God, because the Lord hears us. The Lord can change your plan for funeral clothes into a refreshed body, full of joy and with a renewed purpose. Sing praises, give thanks, and let God renew you!!

Prayer

Lord, I sing praises to you at all times. When I'm on top of the world or when the weight of the world feels heavy on my body, I will sing praises to you. When I'm tired, give me energy. When I'm weak, strengthen me. When I'm sick heal me. You are my light and my life. Lord I trust you to renew me right now.

Rev. Elliott Robinson, JD, MDiv

Associate Minister
Saint Philip AME Church
Atlanta, GA
Executive Director of Creative Tension, a non-profit that gives a voice to people and periods of struggle, forgotten by history (createtension.org).

DAY 9
Renewal: The Nearness of God

Psalm 34:15-19 (KJV)
Psalm 34 is a Psalm of David, when he changed his behavior before Abimelech; who drove him away, and he departed. This account is found in I Samuel 21,22. King David writes this in response to how the Spirit of God led him to be different when his life was in danger. He begins the psalm by declaring: "I will bless the Lord at all times: His praise shall continually be in my mouth" (stanza 1). This is the introductory sentence in how we should approach Jehovah in our times of need, stress, trials, and tribulations. We can be assured, even in the storm, Jehovah is near.

It is reassuring to know that *"the eyes of the Lord are upon the righteous, and his ears are open unto their cry"* (stanza 15). How many times have we been in dire straits and wondered if Jehovah was there? The scripture reminds us as a child of God, not only does he see, but he hears. Can you see King David standing before his enemy and acting unKing-like but knowing the King of Kings sees his behavior! God will make a way of escape for us. *"The face of the Lord is against them that do evil, to cut off the remembrance of them from the earth"* (stanza 16). The all-seeing God is always on the side of the oppressed and afflicted. He is nearer to us than we can imagine or think. Just as God told Pharaoh, these you see today you will see again.

Our faith which brings us into right-relationship with the Father, through his Son, Jesus the Christ is the reason we know the truth of stanza 17-" *The righteous cry, and the Lord heareth, and delivereth them, out of all their troubles."* Often, we see our children fall, and tears begin to stream down their cheeks. Our response is to move swiftly toward them; pick them up; dust them off; and kiss the bruise. This is how Jehovah sees us in keeping us near to him. Whenever our hearts are broken by life's challenges, and we want to throw in the towel, remember God is near. We have many afflictions as a child of the Most-High God, but we also have an assurance of the comforting arms of Jesus and presence of the Comforter to be near. (stanza 18-19).

Prayer

Father God, thank you for being near to me, not just in the good times, but when times are not as good. Draw me nearer blessed Lord. Increase my faith through my tests, trials, tribulations, and storms. In Jesus name, I pray. Amen!

Rev. Gregory C. Nettles
Pastor, Bethel African Methodist Episcopal Church
Camden, AR
12th Episcopal District

DAY 10
Renewal: God Will See to It

Psalm 37:1-11 (NKJV)

Have you ever wondered why those who live a sinful life, seem to enjoy the better things this life has to offer? In this psalm, which is attributed to David, but may have been written by someone else, chooses to focus on this burning contradiction in his understanding about the goodness, grace, and mercy of God. Evil people and workers of iniquity (sinful) are prospering, while the righteous are getting the raw end of the deal. In the observation of the writer, he (I) cannot focus on what they (evil doers) are gaining in this world of sin and shame. He must conclude the judgment of an almighty God who "sits high and looks low. He guides my feet, where ever I may go. Sometimes I just do not understand, I have a Father who can."

Trusting and doing good allows one to have the faith of God to see the situation; also, delighting in the Lord will bring my problems to the place in which I can tell my problems how big my God is. Knowing beyond a shadow of a doubt about my God seeing to it, whatever it may be, is a direct result of my commitment to trusting in an omniscience God who has the answer to the situation before the situation showed up in my life.

What does it mean to "rest" in God? We can take a lesson from the political leader named Daniel but had a relationship with God. When laws are passed to hinder, he persevered long enough to see his enemies be destroyed in front of his eyes. When I know God will see to it, I can keep my emotional temper tantrums from consuming my time, for one day, they (evil doers) will soon be cut off. My spiritual understanding of the strength of meekness, reminds me that I have an inheritance not made by man's hands. I can sleep peacefully during a storm on a raging sea, be thrown in a furnace burning hot enough to melt gold or facing an experienced warrior who is bigger than me physically, but the God in me is greater than the sword in his hand. Know beloved, for sure, God will see to it.

Prayer

Gracious God, thank you for a faith that will not fail nor cause me to doubt your word, which is a lamp unto my feet. Thank you for being my provider despite those around me doing evil and attaining status, positions, and prospering. I will forever praise you, knowing my blessing is on the way. In Jesus name. Amen!

Rev. Gregory C. Nettles
Pastor, Bethel African Methodist Episcopal Church
Camden, AR
12th Episcopal District

DAY 11
God Will Turn It Around

Psalm 37:5-7 (NRSV)

"Commit your way to the LORD; trust in him, and he will act. He will make your vindication shine like the light, and the justice of your cause like the noonday. Be still before the LORD AND wait patiently for him; do not fret over those who prosper in their way, over those who carry out evil devices."

It would be nice to think that police planting evidence and framing suspects only existed in movies and on television, wouldn't it? Unfortunately for Arthur Allan Thomas, those two things are all too real. In 1971, Arthur Thomas was convicted for two murders he did not commit because he had been framed by policemen who had sworn to protect and defend citizens. A couple named Jeanette and Harvey Crewe had been murdered in their home in Waikato, New Zealand. It would later be discovered that the police had planted a cartridge from Thomas's rifle in the couple's garden.

There was finally a royal commission which uncovered the suspicious actions of the police throughout the investigation, which Thomas says includes using things he told them against him. Thomas has been out of prison for more than thirty-five years, but his family is still seeking justice in the form of charges against the police responsible. The two men who fabricated the evidence are now both deceased.

The enemy will do anything to hinder or destroy us. He will mislead people, cause confusion or division. It times like these we need a Savior. When we become weary or when we have been drained by the tricks of the enemy we can put all of our confidence in God.

Don't focus on your pain or your problem but rely on the power of God. Don't allow the enemy to make you feel defeated. Rely on the grace of God. He will pick you up. He will set you free. He will make your life brand new. He will take care of you.

Prayer

Lord thank you for watching over me. When I was in trouble you came to rescue me. I am grateful that you vindicated me. I am grateful that you turned things around in my life. In Jesus Name, I pray. Amen.

Rev. Dr. Roy Jones, Jr
Executive Minister
Saint Philip AME Church
Atlanta, GA

DAY 12
Stay Focus

Psalm 37:7 (NLT)
"Be Still in the presence of the Lord and wait patiently for Him to act. Don't Worry about the evil people who prosper or fret about their wicked schemes."

It was once said that the greatest trick ever played was that the devil convinced the world that he was not real. It is the job of the enemy to keep you from moving and operating in your purpose. The enemy has many tricks and devices to accomplish his mission but the thing that the enemy uses the most and has the biggest impact on you is to affect your focus.

When I was growing up I was introduced to the term "keeping up with the Jones" this is when we look at what other people have and make sure we have what they have, or we make sure we have something better than them. Keeping up with the Jones is a never-ending game of cat and mouse. As technology changes so do the toys, and technology changes what seems like every few months. However, people will break the bank to have the newest and latest toy as they work to outdo each other. As people focus on the latest toy and gadget they lose focus on their purpose and the enemy has successfully delayed you from operating in God purpose.

We are not put here to chase after the latest toy no matter how nice they are. God has called us to arms! He has called us to perform on His behalf and to bring Him glory. We are His spoke persons to the nation. David tells us to be still and be patience as we are in the presence of the Lord. God knows our heart's desire, and nothing would make Him happier then to give us all that we want and more. However, we must first be obedient to His will and instructions that He gives us. One of many promises made on this topic is that if we first seek the kingdom of God then all thing will be given unto us. We must calm our mind and our spirits in the presence of God.

Your life has purpose! It is your job, and your duty to fulfill your purpose for God in this life.

Once we successfully accomplish waiting on God the enemy has another trick to distract us. We see our neighbors prosper as we seem to be stuck because we are waiting on God. Feelings of anger and frustration can creep into our mind and begin to taint our thoughts. Therefore, David tells us not to worry about evil people. Nor fret about the schemes that seem to prosper. If you are busy watching them and allowing yourself to be angry and frustrated, then you are not operating at your best; this allows the enemy to win. You must realize that you are not stuck, in fact you are exactly where God has placed you. If you are where God has placed, you then you are in the right place. Focus on your purpose and not on other people! Success in this life is not gaged by the size of your bank account! Hold your ground! Focus on your purpose and watch God come through for you!

Prayer

Heavenly Father, I need your help to stay focus on the purpose you have given me. I can easily fall into the enemy's traps and get distract by watching others. Please forgive me Lord. I am your servant and I will accomplish all that you have given me to do with your help. Please allow my mind to stay focus on You. Thank You for being patient with me and thank You for your help, I love You, and it is my heart's desire to serve You Lord. Amen

Bro. Jeaune Yarde
Associate Minister
Saint Philip AME Church
Atlanta, GA

DAY 13
A Song and A Prayer

Psalm 42:8 (NRSV)

"By day the Lord commands his steadfast love, and at night his song is within me, a prayer to the God of my life."

When one initially looks at this verse, it is easy to think of day as the literal daylight that we see upon waking each morning. Similarly, we tend to look at night as the literal time of day. However, this verse speaks to us on a deeper level. Metaphorically, day stands for the pleasant and joyous occasions. Likewise, night represents the dark, dismal, and difficult times in our lives. Like most people, when good things happen we are all excited but when "bad" or not so good things happen we start looking around in utter dismay and disbelief. We go through a litany of protestations such as, "I am saved. I am a good person. I go to church. Why is this happening to me?" Yet, this psalm gives us keen insight into understanding what is happening during the positive as well as the negative times.

Who does not hum a song or two during the good experiences of their lives? During the day, there is steadfast love and joy that causes us to abound in praise to God. Despite the night or difficult times, there is still a song for us to sing. This does not necessarily mean you will have an audible song, but it does mean that you will have calm reassurance in your spirit that will see you through the rough patches in life. Now, it is perfectly fine if you do have an actual song in the night. If you need a confidant you might sing, "What a Friend We Have in Jesus." If you are in need of prayer you might sing, "I Must Tell Jesus."

Of particular importance is the fact that the songs we sing are really prayers to our God. The beauty of steadfast love in the day and a song in the night is that God is with us through them all. From the highest apex to the lowest nadir, God is there. Our renewal and rejuvenation through songs and prayers fortify us and strengthen our faith.

Prayer

O God, help us enjoy the glorious days and tempestuous nights that we experience. As we continually walk with You, help us sing a song that reminds us that You are with us every step of the way. Help us remember that You still answer prayers. Amen.

Rev. Pricilla Adams
Minister of Pastoral Care
Saint Philip AME Church
Atlanta, GA

DAY 14
Daily Renewal is Liberating

Psalm 51.10 (NRSV)
"Create in me a clean heart, O God, and renew a right spirit within me."

Life is a complex journey and even nature experiences its own complexities and seasons. As people, we journey through our seasons, acquiring all of the human emotions and acts possible. Eventually our emotions and acts take a toll on us. Like King David, we should purge ourselves and cry out to God for help. To desire spiritual cleanliness is so liberating and fulfilling.

A desire for a clean heart requires renewal. There are renewals on prescriptions, magazines, insurance policies, and warranties to name a few; so why not the spiritual state of our hearts? Not only is a clean heart necessary for a productive relationship with God, but a right spirit that is faithful, true, and unwavering with a steady beat. And so, in obedience to God, we should daily desire this repentance; this renewal is a fresh start.

As humans, we must realize that our thoughts can sometimes become toxic and our physical bodies are overwhelmed with acts unpleasing to God. Restoration is at the heart of God, and as our hearts are being renewed, it is God's desire for us to maintain a steadfast spirit not uncertain in purpose or action, but constant. How through prayer, fasting, repentance, worship and devotion, and by reading God's word a renewed heart becomes anchored. King David needed forgiveness and he desperately sought after it. Likewise, as believers we are to seek God's face for forgiveness, so that He can restore our brokenness and to encourage us so that we can serve others. Service is the heart of God; and a heart that has been renewed is most liberating!

Prayer

Father, thank you for a daily renewal. May I always look to you with a repentant heart, an alert mind, and a steadfast prayer life. Amen.

Rev. Diana Mason Kirk

Associate Minister
Saint Philip A. M. E. Church
240 Chandler Road, S. E.
Atlanta, GA 30317

DAY 15
Make Me New

Psalm 51:10-13 (KJV)

"Create in me a clean heart, O God; and renew a right spirit within me. Cast me not away from thy presence; and take not thy holy spirit from me. Restore unto me the joy of thy salvation; and uphold me with thy free spirit. Then will I teach transgressors thy ways; and sinners shall be converted unto thee."

Depression, disappointment, disillusionment may often be the cause of life's discontentment. We start to believe that there is nothing to hope for and that our prayers are going nowhere. We start to behave as if our God has let us down. We believe that our circumstances will never change.

In the old Testament, David may have felt this way at times when he was in the wilderness running for his life. He may have wondered "Lord, where are you? I am hiding to save myself." David may have felt all alone, and no one can understand what he was going through. His faith may have faltered when it seemed he would be hiding forever.

Like David, we must persevere, keep pushing forward, and believe God can do all things. We must ask God to keep us from despair and desperation, renew our faith and strengthen us. God can and will deliver us from our enemies, we must remain steadfast in our faith under all circumstances and be an encouragement to others.

Prayer

Lord, You, are the master of all creation. Your mercy sustains me, Your love nourishes my soul. Lord, I look to You for comfort and strength during times of trials and hardships. You are the keeper of all things good. Lord, help me to remember to seek Your guidance and wisdom. Lord, help me to accept Your will and understand Your plan for me is greater than my plan for me. Lord, keep me in Your presence and I will show others Your ways and teach them Your laws. Lord, You are my rock and I will seek you always. In the name of Your Son, Jesus, I pray. Amen.

Sister Tammie Dennis
St. James AME Church
Camden, AR

DAY 16
Give me a Willing Spirit

Psalms 51:10-12 (NRSV)

"Create in me a clean heart, O God, and put a new and right spirit within me. Do not cast me away from your presence, and do not take your holy spirit from me. Restore to me the joy of your salvation and sustain in me a willing spirit."

The believer desires renewal to holiness as much as the joy of salvation. He does not pray; Lord preserve me or my reputation. His great concern is to have his corrupt nature changed. He now saw more than ever, what an unclean heart he had and sadly laments it, but sees it is not in his own power to amend it, and therefore begs God to create in him a clean heart, only the one who made the heart can make it new again. To God's power nothing is impossible. By the word of His power as the God of grace we are clean, and we are sanctified. The producing of a holy disposition in a sinner's heart, the forming in his/her a submissive will, a pure imagination, and well-regulated affections is a new creation.

This state of the understanding and heart is a right spirit, conformable to the image and law of our creator. It was in mankind originally, but was lost by the fall, therefore producing it is the renewal of a right spirit. It is begun in regeneration, carried on by progressive sanctification and completed in glory. When the sinner feels this change is necessary, and reads the promise of God to that purpose, he/she begins to ask God for help, and every discovery of his/her remaining sinfulness leads the believer to renew the supplication more earnestly. Renew a right spirit within me: therefore, he prays Lord fix me for the time to come that, I may never in like manner, depart from you.

He prays for the continuance of God's will toward him, and the progress of his good work in him. God's will be done; but Lord rebuke me not in your wrath. Let me have a God to go to in my distress and all shall be well. And that he might never be deprived of God's grace. The thing that David dreaded the most was for the Holy Spirit to withdraw from him. So, he prays, let your Holy Spirit continue with me to prefect the work of my repentance, to prevent my relapse into sin, and to enable me to discharge my duty. He prays for the restoration of Divine comforts and the perpetual communications of Devine grace.

Prayer

Lord by willful sin we forfeit the joy and fellowship that we share with you and we deprive ourselves of the peace that the Holy Spirit affords us. When we find ourselves clouded in despair, and our hopes shaken by our mistakes, help us to remember that those who sow in true repentance shall reap in the joys of God's salvation, when the times of refreshing shall come. Amen

Rev. D'Andrea Daniels
Associate Minister
Saint Philip A.M.E. Church
Atlanta, GA

DAY 17
No Renewal Without Repentance

Psalm 51:10-13 (NRSV)

"Create in me a pure heart, God and make my spirit right again. Do not send me away from you or take your Holy Spirit away from me. Give me back the joy of my salvation. Keep me strong by giving me a willing spirit. Then I will teach your ways to those who do wrong, and sinners will turn back to you."

Create in me is a prayer we all would do well to pray daily and even many times during the day. It is what one must do to stay in communion with God. When David prayed for a clean heart, God answered affirmatively! David at one time had a God-fearing conscience. He remembered his spiritual connection with God that he had experienced even as a young boy with a sling shot, but somehow, he had begun to ignore it. However, he realized that there could be no renewal without repentance. So, David prayed to God and pleaded with Him to turn His eyes from his sin and blot out all his guilt and transgressions.

One may ask the question, "How can one man go from keeping desperately close to and depending on God daily and then become weak and ineffective?" The answer is simply that David started to lose his sense of desperate dependency upon God's presence and God's power in his life. His sinful behavior had taken a toll on his relationship with God and he had become less sensitive to the presence of the Holy Spirit upon him. He had become infected by palace living and succumbed to the downfalls of the prosperity lifestyle.

As believers, like David, we too become infected by the things of this world, and we must repent and seek God daily for a refreshing - asking God to search us and see if there is any wicked way within us. Our lesson learned from David is that God will not reject a heart that wants a RENEWAL in his/her life by the Holy Spirit. Only God has the power to change us, replenish us, and restore us. It is time to seek God's renewal in our lives and be refreshed!

Prayer

Dear Lord, help us to seek your face. We realize that no self-help book or lecture series can renew us or give us a makeover in our lives. We turn to you, this day, asking you to create in us a clean heart --make our spirits right again and keep us close to you. In Jesus' Name. Amen

Rev. John Williams
Associate Minister
Saint Philip AME Church
Atlanta, GA

DAY 18
Justice

Psalm 94:12-15 (NLT)

"Joyful are those you discipline, LORD, those you teach with your instructions. You give them relief from troubled times until a pit is dug to capture the wicked. The LORD will not reject his people; he will not abandon his special possession. Judgment will again be founded on justice, and those with virtuous hearts will pursue it."

When our children make mistakes, we encourage and redirect them. When they do the wrong things and we have taught them differently, we correct and discipline them. When they are lost or confused, we try to point the way.

God comes to our aid when we have been blindsided, misguided or when we sin or make bad decisions. Even if we are struggling, facing conflict, have been crushed or have financial crisis, God will come to our aid.

Even if we have suffered wrongfully or if we have been abused, God can help us. When we face injustice, or deal with corruption, God has the last Word.

Prayer

Lord, we praise you for Jesus who endured shame and injustice. We thank you for the power over injustice and the power of Renewal by way of the cross and resurrection, in Jesus Name. Amen

Rev. Dr. Roy Jones, Jr.
Executive Minister
Saint Philip AME Church
Atlanta, GA

DAY 19
Renewal

Psalm 103:1-2 (NRSV)
"Bless the Lord, O my soul, and all that is within me. Bless His holy name. Bless the Lord, O my soul and do not forget all his benefits."

The Psalmist David in the 103rd division begins by "stirring up" himself to praise the Lord for God's favor to him. With all that David had encountered and experienced, with all the deficits in his own spiritual life, and with all his remembrance of his many past failures, he recognized his need for RENEWAL - restoration of spiritual strength! So David summons to his mind the things (mercies, benefits and promises) that God has done for him and given to him in spite of himself: David illuminates that God forgives all our sins and iniquities; He heals all our diseases; He redeems our lives from destruction; He loads us with love and mercy; He is slow to anger and gives us space to repent; He satisfies us with good things, and He recovers us from our decays and fills us with new life and joy.

Like David, we must recognize our need for renewal and "stir up" ourselves and our own souls to praise the Lord. In doing so, we do not forget all His kindness towards us and we call to our own remembrance what the Lord has already done for us. RENEWAL excites us. RENEWAL is the alpha and omega of all our serving. RENEWAL causes us to not only stir up ourselves, but others. RENEWAL refreshes, restores, makes new, and replenishes. It commands us to Bless the Lord - for all that we are. It commands us to Praise the Lord with everything within us - It commands us to Praise the Lord with our whole being and never ever forget all His kindness. Stir it up--stir up your praise and Bless the Lord!

Prayer

Father, we thank you for direction in renewal. You have not dealt with us according to our sins or given us what we deserve. We ask that you help us to lead disciplined, consistent lives in our study, walk, and worship with You. Stir us up, Lord, and we give you all the glory.

Rev. Carolyn Williams
Associate Minister
Saint Philip AME Church
Atlanta, GA

DAY 20
Rescued with the Word

Psalm 119:71-72 (KJV)

"It is good for me that I have been afflicted; that I might learn thy statutes. The law of thy mouth is better unto me than thousands of gold and silver."

How wonderful is the word of God? Even during hard times and difficult situations the word of God is a lamp unto our feet. David relied on God's word to keep him throughout his life. He operated under the power of God from the time he was a boy through adulthood. Every issue, every trial, every battle David depended on God. David was not perfect, but he sought out the Lord all his days. Psalm 103 verse 1 and 2 in the Complete Jewish Bible reflects the relationship David had with God; it reads, Bless Adonai, my soul, everything in me, bless His holy name! Bless Adonai, my soul, and forget none of His benefits.

No one has a perfect life, but we have to know where the Source of our comfort comes from. Seek God's face in His word. There is wisdom in His word, there is love in His word, there is reassurance in His word. The word of the Lord is the life-raft on our lifelong journey, it rescues us and gives us solace.

Prayer

Lord, Adonai bless you. Bless You from sunup to sunset. Bless You O Lord for keeping me through my problems and troubles. Lord, I seek Your face in all things. You, O Lord are the master of every good thing. Thank you, Father, thank you for making straight the path to You. Thank you, O Lord, for being the source of my strength and Your laws for lighting my way. Thank you, O Lord, for who You are. In the matchless name of Your Son, Yeshua HaMashiach, Jesus Christ. Amen

Sister Tammie Dennis
St. James AME Church
Camden, AR

DAY 21
Self-Check: The Prelude to Spiritual Renewal

Psalm 139:23-24 (NIV)
"Search me, God, and know my heart; test me and know my anxious thoughts. See if there is any offensive way in me and lead me in the way everlasting."

In the game of basketball, there are a multitude of terms to describe different types of players. One of the terms that come to mind is the term "self-check". This describes a player that is not an offensive threat whatsoever. They cannot score a basket if life depended on it. However, in the game of life, self-check can have some qualities that can be not only lifesaving to the Christian, it can also be soul saving towards the path of spiritual renewal.

Psalms 139: 23-24 is poised to make you meditate and put yourself on the sideline and cause you to go back to the spiritual gym and work on Prayer, Study and Meditation of God's Word. The prelude to spiritual renewal is to work your way out of a spiritual slump. It takes a convinced, convicted and connected Christian to want to experience the fullness of God.

It is a challenging world that we live in. There are times when life can have more ebbs than flows. It is then that the Christian that is in the ebb of life call on the Lord to search them, know their heart, test and know their thoughts, and lead them to the everlasting. When this happens through Prayer, Study and Meditation, self-check becomes soul saving instead of life threatening. This is the prelude to spiritual renewal any and every time.

Prayer

In This Season, Lord of Spiritual Renewal, we ask for the Spirit of humbleness as we seek grace and mercy as you search us to renew us. Lord You know us and now test us so that you may lead us to your Glory. It is in Jesus' Name that we pray. Amen.

Rev. Kurbe L. Newsom
Senior Pastor
St. Paul A.M.E. Church
Jonesboro, AR
Arkansas Conference
12th Episcopal District

DAY 22
God Heals the Brokenhearted

Psalm 147:3 (NLT)
"He heals the brokenhearted and bandage their wounds."

If your heart has been broken, you can be renewed. The longer we avoid a problem, the worse it becomes. Everyone that experience growth and development will experience pain. Pain can take us to the place we never desired to be. However, pain can also help us find a way out of something that could have destroyed us. Pain humbles us and drives us to prayer.

When a relationship has gone sour, or when we experience heartbreaking losses, the pain may seem unbearable. We must understand that through pain or hard times God shows Himself strong. God redirects us. In our most unfavorable or unfortunate circumstances, God can heal the broken hearted and bandage their wounds.

Pain teaches us to depend on the Lord. Jesus is the example of enduring pain. Jesus is the example that God renews. Jesus is the example of hope in the darkest of times. The life of Jesus reminds us that the pain is worth the progress.

Prayer

Lord, your grace is sufficient, and your mercy endures forever. Thanks for healing the brokenhearted. In Jesus Name I pray.

Rev. Dr. Roy Jones, Jr.
Executive Minister
Saint Philip AME Church
Atlanta, GA

DAY 23
Word that Gives Wisdom

Proverbs 1:33 (NKJV)
"But whoever listens to me will dwell safely, and will be secure, without fear of evil."

If you stare in the face of fear, with evil all around you, know that the Word of God according to 2 Timothy 1:7 NKJV, *"For God has not given us a spirit of fear, but of power and of love and of a sound mind."* The Word of God causes even the devil to tremble at the Name of Jesus.

Words are to be spoken and heard to produce an understanding. God's Word gives wisdom, it increases learning, knowledge and corrects us as well. As we hold to Gods Word, it will lead us to a place of safety, it will lead us to greener pastures, it will lead us beside the still waters of peace.

So, when we listen, and obey the Word of God, we can have the assurance of safety during the storm. When we obey the Word of God, it gives wisdom to avoid some of the storms that we may cause. When we obey the Word of God, it will align us with the will of God.

Prayer

Lord, help us to dwell in Your Word where there is safety, wisdom, knowledge, instructions and learning. Order our steps in the Word dear Lord and help me to stay away from the very appearance of evil. In Jesus Name, Amen.

Jeffery C. Fields, Pastor
New Haven MBC
Camden, AR

DAY 24
Wisdom for Renewal

Proverbs 2:16-22 (NIV)

"Wisdom will save you also from the adulterous woman, from the wayward woman with her seductive words, who have left the partner of her youth and ignored the covenant she made before God. Surely her house leads down to death and her path to the spirit of the dead. None who go to her return or attain the path of life. Thus, you will walk in the ways of good and keep to the path of the righteous. For the up right will live in the land, and the blameless will remain in it; but the wicked will be cut off from the land and the unfaithful will be ripped up."

Renewal and rebirth cannot occur without ending as the new year's crops cannot only be planted and flourish in the decay of the last year. Careers and relationships also have their cycles of birth, growth, and death-to be followed by rebirth and renewal of the cycle.

Choose wisdom and renew yourself to live as Christ has promised to the faithful, "new life, growth, and a change in cycle. John 10:10 says, "the thief cometh not, but for to steal, and to kill, and to destroy: I am come that they might have life, and that you might have it more abundantly." (Jonathan Lockwood Haie)

Prayer

I pray for wisdom, knowledge, and understanding. Grant me, Oh God, the spirit of each of these words as I engage in renewal and transformation. Allow me to draw closer to your ways so that my life will be full of wisdom and as fresh as the warm summer dew. AMEN

Rev. Carlton Gibson
Associate Minister
Saint Philip AME Church
Atlanta, GA

DAY 25
Trust in the Lord

Proverbs 3:5-6 (NIV)
"Trust in the LORD with all thine heart; and lean not unto thine own understanding. In all thy ways acknowledge him, and he shall direct thy paths."

Solomon understood what many of us still need to learn. Our lives will be radically different when we completely and comprehensively put our trust in the Lord. When we put our trust in GOD and acknowledge HIM as Lord of our lives, HE responds by directing our paths.

Antithetical to this complete and comprehensive trust in the lord is the unsustainability of human independence absent of His Divine assistance. Our very existence is dependent on HIS Divine Grace. We simply cannot make it through this life without the Lord. We have no hope in this life without the Holy help of our GOD. I have lived long enough and through enough to acknowledge that it was the Lord that made the way. It was the Lord that kept me and protected me. It was the Lord who in the words of Marvin Sapp, held me close so I wouldn't let go. Likewise, Solomon has lived long enough and through enough to know for himself that it was the Lord who had "directed his path."

Literally, Solomon is saying when we put our trust in GOD and depend on him, HE will remove any and all obstacles in our lives that seek to prevent us from living the life HE has designed and desires for us. What a blessed promise and wonderful reminder that even as the situations and circumstances of our lives change, we should keep trusting in the Lord. Through the transitions of life---keep trusting. Through the bouts of illness---keep trusting. Through the moments of uncertainty and calamity---keep trusting. I am a living witness that when we trust in the Lord, HE removes obstacles, opponents and opposition that block our paths. When we trust God, HE lifts our burdens and destroys the strongholds in our lives. When we trust in the Lord, we are guaranteed some Holy Help on this journey called life.

Prayer

Lord grant us the wisdom to trust in you with all that we are and all that we have. Make us sensitive to your providential care that we may fully comprehend what is the length and width, height and depth of your love. Help us to understand that if we completely and comprehensively put our trust in you that you will order our steps and indeed direct our paths. And help us to keep trusting you through the twists and turns of life that we may be able to testify with integrity like the hymnist, "I will trust in the Lord until I die." In your name we pray, Amen.

Rev. Dr. Paul Flowers
Pastor, Mount Zion Baptist Church
Mechanicville, VA
PDF Ministries

DAY 26
Knowledge, Understanding, and Wisdom

Proverbs 4:7 (NIV)
"The beginning of wisdom is this: Get wisdom. Though it cost all you have, get understanding"

When my two boys were little, we established a Friday night tradition of ordering take-out or fast food and renting a movie for an evening of entertainment. On this particular Friday, my funds were limited, and I had to explain to them that we would be eating left-overs and watching a repeat of movies. To my surprise, my youngest son responded like this: "Momma, I've got a great idea. Just go to that machine at the bank, put your card in and punch in your numbers; it will give you some money." As I smiled with laughter, I realized that he had knowledge that money could be extracted from the ATM machine but lacked understanding that the magical bank card was connected to a bank account with no money.

The definition of knowledge is simply gaining information. Understanding means, the ability to comprehend and wisdom is the application of knowledge and understanding. Knowledge, understanding and wisdom are often used by God (together) in communication with humanity. These three words used are related and are somehow interconnected. The wisest man in the Bible by the name of Solomon was asked by God, "if you can have anything, what would it be?" His response was "a wise an understanding mind...".

I believe Solomon understood that having information only was pointless unless you understood its possibilities, use and potential. And if you understand its possibilities and potential and yet don't apply it, then there is no growth. Therefore, the ultimate goal in life is wisdom, but the most important goal is understanding. At what cost would you give to gain all three?

Prayer

Creator and sustaining God, thank you for gifts of knowledge, understanding and wisdom. Help us to use these gifts appropriately and timely to glorify you in all that we do. Let your will be done, in the name of Jesus, Amen.

Rev. Alexia Ford
Associate Minister
Saint Philip AME Church
Atlanta, GA

DAY 27
Guard Your Heart

Proverbs 4:23-24 (NIV)
"Above all else, guard your heart, for everything you do flows from it. Keep your mouth free of perversity; keep corrupt talk far from your lips."

To produce Godly fruits such as joy, love and kindness toward others, it is critical that believers guard their hearts, and allow God to guide our paths so that our plans can be established and succeed. The heart and the mind direct all our actions and they should get guarded appropriately from any ungodly thoughts, beliefs, and ideas to avoid any spiritual downfall. Also, what comes from our hearts brings the issues of life meaning that we should center our hearts on God to produce excellent fruits or issues that we need such as self-control, patience, goodness, joy, faithfulness, and love. When one centers his/her heart on flesh, they find themselves in sinful acts.

As well as our hearts, we should control our mouth. For the mouth can destroy or build. It can lead one to sin in various ways such as lying, planning evil, cursing, or speaking evil things. Therefore, we should learn to speak life over ourselves, as well as others. Additionally, we should control our eyes to look ahead to view what God has placed ahead, and to see all the good that God has planned for our lives. Therefore, guard your heart, tongue, and eyes that we might not sin against God.

Prayer

Dear Heavenly Father, we come before your throne of mercy and grace asking that you will grant us the wisdom and guidance we need to guard our heart, our tongues, and our eyes that we may not sin against you or your kingdom. Lord, we ask that you fill our hearts with love; our tongues with words of life, and our eyes with visions that will build your kingdom. In Jesus name, Amen

Rev. Sharon Adair-Harden
Pastor, Greater St. Paul AME Church
Austell, GA

DAY 28
Guard the Affections of Your Heart

Proverbs 4:23 (HCSB)
"Guard your heart above all else, for it is the source of life."
(Holman Christian Standard Bible)

I am persuaded that one of the key reasons why so many of us miss the mark to receive from God the equipment which we ought to be receiving lies in the fact that our emotions and our thoughts are not properly connected.

Do you catch yourself repeatedly praying for possessions you never obtain? I don't mean belongings about which there may be some hesitation, but things you absolutely know the almighty desires to give you-friendship, happiness, reconciliation, understanding, perseverance, and so on. Maybe your thoughts are asking for one thing and your soul another. You see, it is possible to want something with the awareness which is not supported by the mood. The notice is much easier part of the behavior to deal with than the core, but, as our text states: "Guard your heart...for it is the source of life."

We miss the mark to accept God, because we are not examining our hearts out of a completely adjusted character. God is not just paying attention to our confrontations; He is attending to us.

Prayer

O Father, help me to be complete in Christ. Lord, help me to be as excited to reach up higher to You. Amen.

Rev. Dr. Gene B. Moore, Jr.
Pastor, New Life Baptist Church
320 Park Avenue
Piqua, Ohio 45356

DAY 29
Start New, Seek God

Proverbs 8:35-36 (KJV)
"For whoever finds Me finds life and obtains favor from the Lord; For whoso findeth me findeth life and shall obtain favour of the LORD."

Have you gotten yourself in a jam? Are you operating under your will? Are you plowing forward on your timetable? How is this working out for you? Do you find yourself frustrated, wondering why things aren't going your way? Maybe, it's time to stop and listen. Do you hear that still, small voice telling you, you've forgotten to seek My will?

Our day to day lives revolve around getting as much done as possible. We forget to go to God to find out how to go forward, when to go forward, with whom we should go forward. So, let's take a minute to stop and ask God what it is He wants us to do, how He wants it done, and when to do what He wants. We find that maybe His ways and His will can take us farther and the results are eternal.

Prayer

Blessed are You, O Lord, Creator of the universe. Thank you for Your guidance and patience. Lord, thank You for planning my days and providing a way for me to follow You. Father, help me to understand Your will for me is greater than I can imagine. Thank you, Lord, for Your loving-kindness. Thank You for giving me the opportunity to do Your will. In Jesus name, Amen.

Sister Tammie Dennis
St. James AME Church
Camden, AR

DAY 30
Anxiety

Proverbs 12:25 (NRSV)
"Anxiety weighs down the human heart, but a good word cheers it up."

We ask someone, "How was your weekend?" and they begin with a heavy sigh. We scroll through our social media feed or news channels and go from feeling upbeat to being afraid to leave the house, walk down the street or just sit in a coffee shop. Instead of resting in the protection of God's arms, we feel like we're on a constant state of high alert. Pressure...stress...tension...anxiety...all weigh down our heart, literally and figuratively.

The human heart is our engine. When the heart is not right, then we become susceptible to issues like high blood pressure, heart disease or stroke. But there's a way to off-set that anxiety, good words. When I see the phrase "good words," I think of both the words we hear and the words we speak.

During this time of renewal, think about the words you speak. In fact, go one step earlier and be mindful of the thoughts you think. What are you thinking about and how does that measure up to the "good words" that will give you cheer? Whether it's friends, family or media, monitor who speaks and pours into your heart. Anxiety will not weigh down our hearts because we are committed to a life of good words!

Prayer

Lord, we submit our hearts to you. We commit our mouths and ears to speak and receive words of good cheer. During this season of renewal, we are committed to allowing your peace, which passes all understanding, to be our comfort, our guide and our source of cheer. In Jesus' name we pray, Amen!!

Rev. Elliott Robinson, JD, MDiv
Associate Minister
Saint Philip AME Church
Atlanta, GA
Executive Director of Creative Tension, a non-profit that gives a voice to people and periods of struggle, forgotten by history (createtension.org).

DAY 31
Renewed Hope

Proverbs 13:12 (NLT)
"Hope deferred makes the heart sick, but a dream fulfilled is a tree of life."

God can and will assist those who have lost hope or have lost their way. God can renew our hope through his loving kindness and patience. When you feel defeated ask God to "Renew you Hope."

God can and will reveal Himself to us. We may feel tired and worn-out, but help is on the way. God will Renew our hope. We have a God that loves us and will deliver us. Speak life. No more depression. No more confusion. No more waiting. God is in the processing of Renewing Our Hope." Hallelujah, Thank you Lord.

Prayer

Lord, help those who are going through tough times. Help them to feel your presences and to realize you will continue to walk with them. Lord, help them see that whatever they are going through is only a test. Help them to feel confident that you are a God who Renews and besides you there is no other. You have planned the length of the test as well as the depth. Lord, have mercy, and Renew right now, In Jesus Name. Amen.

Rev. Dr. Roy Jones, Jr.
Executive Minister
Saint Philip AME Church
Atlanta, GA

DAY 32
Renewed Peace

Proverbs 16:7 (NKJV)
"When a man's ways please the LORD, He makes even his enemies to be at peace with him."

Be encouraged today. Continue to live in a way that pleases God. Be obedient to the Word of God. Be patient and kind with others. Even when you are attacked by your enemies don't be afraid and be willing to forgive. Because you are pleasing to God, He will make your enemies be at peace with you.

If you haven't pleased those around you, just make sure you please God. God will give us "Renewed Peace." When there is no one to turn remember you can turn to the God of Peace. When you have done all you can do, trust God to give you "Renewed Peace."

Prayer

Lord, we pause to thank you for caring for us. We thank you Lord for listening to our complaints. We thank you Lord for your compassion and understanding. Lord, we stand on your Word, which declares that you will "make our enemies be at peace with us."

Rev. Dr. Roy Jones, Jr.
Executive Minister
Saint Philip AME Church
Atlanta, GA

DAY 33
Educated and Foolish

Proverb 17:16 (ESV)
"Why should a Fool have money in his hand to buy wisdom when he has no sense?"

I was in that period as a parent when my children were old enough to make their own decisions. Father knows best or, so you think because of your own personal 'been there done that' growing pains that history alone equips in your insight to foresee some of the potential danger and the pitfalls that lay in wait for the unsuspecting or the ill advised. There is a difference between education and learning. Education is taught in the schools, Learning is taught in the home. That is why all around us today we see some clearly identifiable educated fools. They truly never received or subscribed to any true learning. We can only be renewed when we know the difference.

In our text this "price" (KJV) can be any resource; money, riches, gifts or opportunities to gain or "to reach" whatever potential there is or could be achieved. Remember in all our getting we are to first get some understanding. What truly is gained if a person squanders all of these things for hopes of being esteemed by the corruptible of and in this world around them? Be it the Arrogance of Entitlement or the Blinding and Binding by the Bling. Surly the temporary, best of right now, can only to end up like the parable of the man who had one talent and did nothing worthwhile with it so in the end it was taken from him.

Prayer

Father God help us to keep our focus on the eternal while we labor here on earth. As we walk in our purpose, block out anything that might distract us or lead us away from the straight and narrow path that points us to you. Renew in us the right spirit each and every moment. And plant in our hearts that it all for your glory to build your kingdom so that that you alone will gain honor and the praise. AMEN

Rev. Melvin Butler
Associate Minister
Saint Philip AME Church
Atlanta, GA

DAY 34
Take Your Medicine

Proverbs 17:22 (NKJV)
"A merry heart does good, like medicine, but a broken spirit dries the bones."

It has been said, "The heart is the spiritual center of our emotions." Consequently, God permits humans to display an array of emotions and feelings that are selectively conditions of the heart. To be exact, God promises us a new heart. His prescription is never wrong. Today's proverb promotes merriment, laughter, cheer, happiness, and joy as good medicine. However, the broken spirit doesn't always appreciate or accept these prescriptions. This type of heart may often replace motives with evil thoughts and actions.

God warns us that seeking happiness through sin is wrong. When ingested, sin is bitter poison that leads to eternal damnation. The non-believer's bones will remain broken, brittle and dry. The hidden and unknown diagnoses regarding this type of heart can only be cured and surgically removed by God. An antidote or good dose of God's miraculous medicine will heal a sin sick soul and make the wounded whole.

Through God's grace, the merry heart can witness to lost souls. The "Great Physician's" office visits delivers laughter, happiness, and joy. Jesus offers eternal healing. Upon Jesus' return, the final appointment ends by rejoicing and praising God's Holy name throughout eternity. To live a healthy spiritual, physical, and emotional life, one must ingest, digest and apply sweet medication which is the "Word of God" daily.

Prayer

Heavenly Father, create in me a clean heart and renew the right spirit within me. Send a fresh anointing of new medication so my heart will exemplify love, joy, peace and happiness. Knowing that the joy of the Lord is my strength, allows me to open my heat in praise and adoration to You. Gladly, I receive the best medicine You have to offer me through Jesus Christ our Savior and Lord. Amen.

Reverend Ina Kay Broomfield,
Associate Minister
Bethel AME Church
600 North Cedar
North Little Rock, AR 72114
12th Episcopal District

DAY 35
Blessed

Proverbs 18:21 (NRSV)

"Death and life are in the power of the tongue, and those who love it will eat its fruits."

Often the words people say about us and to us become true. We cannot yield to tongues that speak negativity into our lives. We cannot and will not accept negative words and words of discouragement in our families, faith, and future. We refuse to accept words that cause fear and torment in our lives. We will be on top and not the bottom.

We are sons and daughters of Almighty God. We are awesome. We have a bright future. We are courageous. We are destined for greatness. We are blessed and highly favored. We are intelligent. We shall prosper and be in good health. We are strong. We are victorious.

Our children will earn college degrees, be saved and live a righteous life. Our grandchildren will be leaders in our communities, universities, hospitals, and law firms. Our children and grandchildren will be successful entrepreneurs.

Prayer

Lord, we thank you for grace and mercy. Lord, we thank you that we are loved and forgiven. Lord, we thank you that we are saved and delivered. Lord we thank you that we are the head and not the tail. In Jesus Name, we give you the praise, honor and glory for all blessings.

Rev. Dr. Roy Jones, Jr.
Executive Minister
Saint Philip AME Church
Atlanta, GA

DAY 36
Teaching Your Youth Well

Proverbs 22:6 (KJV)
"Train up a child in the way he should go, and when he is old he will not depart from it."

In life, we, as human beings, often stray from the path of Christianity. During the course of one's life, there are many side roads that an individual can choose to go down instead of the straight and the narrow. If we are trained in the Christian doctrines and raised up in Christianity, I believe that what we, as individuals, have been taught will always stay with us such as what the Bible states concerning excessive drinking, drugging, and fornication. Through our trials and tribulations, the lessons of Christ are never far away. Generally, after being in the secular world, which we cannot escape, the training that we have received in our younger years, begins to have an impact in our later years. We come full circle with the teachings of Christ. The training and discipline received as a child seems to permeate our consciousness when we have been through the trials of life. As Proverbs 22:6 states *"And when he is old he will not depart from it."* In closing, without this training, we are even more vulnerable to the temptations of the secular world and are open prey for Satan.

Rev. Dr. Derrick Thorpe, Sr.
Academic Dean
Carolina Christian College
Winston-Salem, NC
Pastor, First Baptist Church
Graham, NC

DAY 37
Good Government and Bad Government

Proverbs 29:1-2 (NKJV)

"He who is often rebuked, and hardens his neck, will suddenly be destroyed, and that without remedy. When the righteous are in authority, the people rejoice; But when a wicked man rules, the people groan."

The good leaders of people collapse; society are more likely to monitor complete ethical values. The sensible know that the inspiring will eventually decrease. By contrast, if the top influential in administration and professional are immoral, that dishonesty will network unfortunate to the deepest section of humanity. Proverbs 29:1 risks that one generation, by some resources, the good in detail will tumble. Countries simple correction, just like teenagers and employers (29:1); each desires training, improvement, and even the risk of chastisement or restriction when the first two is not observed.

Verse 2 summarizes the partial. When the world is respectable, people are content; when sinful directions, humanity is depressed. The proverbs about leaders are like those that express of the prosperous of the honorable and the impressive, presenting that controls developed an atmosphere that is totally touched by all the societies. While this cry to justice drives reachable to all the public, a class of filter-down model of honesty is also at effort in the proverbs about the corrective character of the sovereign. Knowledge and foolishness are never practiced in seclusion, but their properties are mainly distinct when accomplished by someone in power.

In our day, we may have grown a bit too cynical about our expectations of leaders, believing that a certain amount of savvy requires some level of moral compromise as well. If national security is threatened, it is better to violate the civil rights of a few to ensure safety for the many. If a leader helps the economy get off the ground, why should we make a judgment on that leader's personal life?

Prayer

O Father, astute leader is like a clever father, or manager, who does all required to impart, be truthful, and contain. We make a difference between the morals of the territory and the kingdom that frontrunners façade every day. You will offer us the understanding to recognize between a talent which is all-purpose and one that is precise. Amen.

Rev. Dr. Gene B. Moore, Jr.
Pastor
New Life Baptist Church
320 Park Avenue
Piqua, Ohio 45356

DAY 38
Renewal Through Loving Kindness

Proverbs 25:21-22

"If your enemies are hungry, give them bread to eat; and if they are thirsty, give them water to drink; for you will heap coals of fire on their heads, and the LORD will reward you."

We cannot control how people treat us, but we can control how we treat people. At times, it seems difficult to express loving kindness towards those who have treated us like enemies. However, by the grace and commandment of God we are expected to love our enemies. We are to offer food and water if they are hungry or thirsty.

Bring your enemies to a sense of comfort by renewing them with the physical things they lack. Forgive your enemies, and God can touch their hearts and minds. Minister to those who are in a dark or rough place. Be kind and God will reward you.

Prayer

Lord give us compassion for those who can't find their way. Lord, help us to make the most of each opportunity to be a blessing to our enemies. Our Father and our God help us to be light in darkness. In Jesus Name with a genuine concern for others we pray. Amen.

Rev. Dr. Roy Jones, Jr.
Executive Minister
Saint Philip AME Church
Atlanta, GA

DAY 39
Renewal and Refuge in God's Word

Proverbs 30:5 (NRSV)
"Every word of God proves true; he is a shield to those who take refuge in him."

Each morning I wake up, I feel Renewed because I made it through another night, to start another day's journey. I start each day with prayer and scripture reading. I know without a doubt that I must be renewed for whatever I must face. I know that God's Word will Renew me throughout the day. Because of God's Word I feel as if I can conquer the world. There's nothing like the assurance I gain from reading and relying on the Word of God for Renewal. Even in the most challenging or difficult part of a day, I know that God is my Refuge. Because of God's Word, and the way He has protected me in the past, I know that He's a Shield. He protects me, and He covers me with His Power and Protection like no other.

Prayer

Father, thank you for Renewal through Your Word. Whatever we need and feel in our hearts, we can find comfort, strength, and Renewal in Your Word. Lord bring a calm assurance on this day. Remind us that You are our Refuge, shield, and strength. Lord, remind us that you will never leave us or forsake us. I pray that we are motivated to spend more time in your Word.

Rev. Dr. Roy Jones, Jr.
Executive Minister
Saint Philip AME Church
Atlanta, GA

DAY 40
Renewal with Purpose

Proverbs 31:8-9 (NRSV)
"Speak out for those who cannot speak, for the rights of all the destitute. Speak out, judge righteously, defend the rights of the poor and needy."

When power or positions are misused, the poor and needy seem to be helpless and hopeless. So many leaders today abuse or misuse their authority. Leaders seem to prosper while the average person, or the less fortunate often suffer, spend time in courts, jails or prisons, or can never seem to rise from unfair and unrighteous treatment.

God warned Israel in Deuteronomy 17 and in 1 Samuel 8:10-22, that kings often use their power and position to benefit themselves. These leaders accumulated horses, wives, silver, and gold and they had no regard for the law of God or the people. They abused their power and treated the people unjustly.

Even today leaders have used their power and position to gain wealth. They have abused the poor and neglected to help the weak and unlearned. God has called us to power and positions today, to stand against the evils of our time. King Lemuel's mother reminded her son that as a leader and King, he was obligated to speak out, judge righteously, defend the rights of the poor and needy.

As Children of God we have a purpose in renewing those who have lost hope. We have a purpose to renew those who are helpless and are being oppressed. Let's seek justice. We are challenged to focus on God's purpose rather than our own. We must use our positions, influence, and resources to accomplish the mission of Renewal.

Prayer

Our Father and our God, we ask that you have mercy upon those who have been unjustly treated. We ask that you have mercy on the poor and the needy. Lord, we pray that leaders who have been appointed, elected and ordained to serve would stand. We pray for courage to speak out, to love and to do justly. Bless us in all our endeavors to do the lord's will. In Jesus Name, we pray. Amen.

Rev. Dr. Roy Jones, Jr.
Executive Minister
Saint Philip AME Church
Atlanta, GA

ABOUT THE AUTHOR

Reverend Dr. Roy Jones, Jr.

Dr. Jones was born December 5, 1967 in Camden, Arkansas to the late Roy and Alice (McBride) Jones. He was raised in Stephens, Arkansas, 17 miles south of his birthplace. He is the youngest of six children.

As a young child, Dr. Jones was baptized and joined New Union AME Church under the leadership of Rev. Irvin Adair. He was educated in the Stephens' Public Schools system. After graduating High School in 1986, he joined the United States Army where he retired, as an E-8/ Master Sergeant, after serving twenty-three years, He and his wife, the former Angela Green, have been married for over twenty-five years and are the parents of four daughters, Kemyasha, Atavia, Olivia, & Iona. Dr. Jones has one granddaughter, Naami.

He is a born-again Christian who loves the Lord and the ministry for which he has been called. The African Methodist Episcopal Church ordained him Itinerant Elder and Dr. Jones began his pulpit ministry on May 1, 1997, returning to his home church, New Union A.M.E. Church in Stephens, AR.

He has served throughout the connection, as the Youth Pastor of Visitors Chapel A.M.E. Church in El Paso, TX, as Minister of Evangelism, Coordinator of Men's Ministry and Assistant Pastor at Bethel AME Church in Pittsburgh, PA, as an associate minister at Bethel A.M.E. Church in West Memphis, AR, as Minister of Evangelism at Bethel A.M.E. Church in Copiague, New York; and pastoring the following charges: Payne Chapel A.M.E. Church in Canonsburg, PA, St. Paul A.M.E. Church in Tuckerman, AR, Bethel A.M.E. Church in Batesville, AR, St. James A.M.E. Church, Camden, AR, Avery Chapel A.M.E. Church in Oklahoma City, OK, and Bethel A.M.E. Church in Little Rock, AR. On August 1, 2017 Dr. Jones became the Executive Minister for Saint Philip A.M.E. Church in Atlanta, GA, where Rev. William D. Watley Ph.D., is the Senior Pastor.

Dr. Jones was elected Delegate for the 2012 and 2016 General Conference of the A.M.E. Church. He is a writer for The Secret Chamber, A Daily Devotion Guide by the Department of Church Growth & Development of the AME Church. Dr. Jones is also the author of *Messages for the Young Adults/Teens/Youth, Lessons Learned from the Book of Deuteronomy, Advancing the Kingdom, Divine Revelation for Divine Restoration, The Cost of Discipleship, The Evidence of Discipleship (Mercy), 40 Days Alone with God: Meditations for Spiritual Renewal I & II, It's Praying Time Because Prayer Still Works and Rescue and Restoration of an African American Community through Education: Leading from the Church.*

Dr. Jones received the Dr. Martin Luther King, Jr. Faith Leadership Award on February 17, 2017 presented by the Arkansas Democratic Black Caucus. He received the 12th Episcopal District African Methodist Episcopal Church 2016 God First Legacy of Leadership Award Outstanding Service and Commitment to Church and Community; Clergy of the Year for Outstanding Achieve for Contributions made to the Lay Organization of the African Methodist Episcopal Church on June 13, 2014. He received an award for his Dedicated Service to the Western District of the Oklahoma State Conference on August 17, 2013.

Dr. Jones attended Pierce College, Fort Lewis, WA; Beecher Lectures at Beeson Divinity School in Birmingham, AL; Proclaimers Place, under the leadership of Dr. Joel Gregory, Central Texas College in Killeen, TX; Austin Peay State University in Clarksville, TN; and Park College in Parkville, MO. He earned an Associate of Arts from Southern Arkansas University Tech in Camden AR., a Bachelor of Science from Excelsior College in Albany, NY, a Master of Divinity from Anchor Theological Seminary of Texarkana, AR, a Master of Arts in Religion (Pastoral Counseling) and a Master in Religious Education (Chaplaincy) at Liberty University,

Lynchburg, VA., and a Doctor of Ministry degree (Preaching & Leadership)- Dissertation: *Rescue and Restoration of an African American Community through Education: Leading from the Church* from United Theological Seminary, Dayton, OH.

BOOK REVIEW

40 Days Alone with God: Meditations for Renewal III

Why now is the perfect time to get Dr. Roy Jones's book? This resource is a goldmine when it comes to growing deeper in the Lord. He gives you present day practicality. He focuses on meditations for renewal such as:

- A Prepared Heart
- Start Singing
- Renewal: The Nearness of God
- Guard Your Heart

I believe this resource is designed for you to enhance your relationship with God. You need this book. It makes for excellent devotional for leaders and laity. I think you're going to thoroughly enjoy this gem of a book.

Rev. Dr. Derrick Thorpe, Sr.
Carolina Christian College
Office of the Academic Dean
4209 Indiana Ave. Winston-Salem, NC 27105

Made in the USA
Middletown, DE
22 July 2021